Animals Around the World

I can draw!

Animals Around the World

Learn to draw exotic animals step by step!

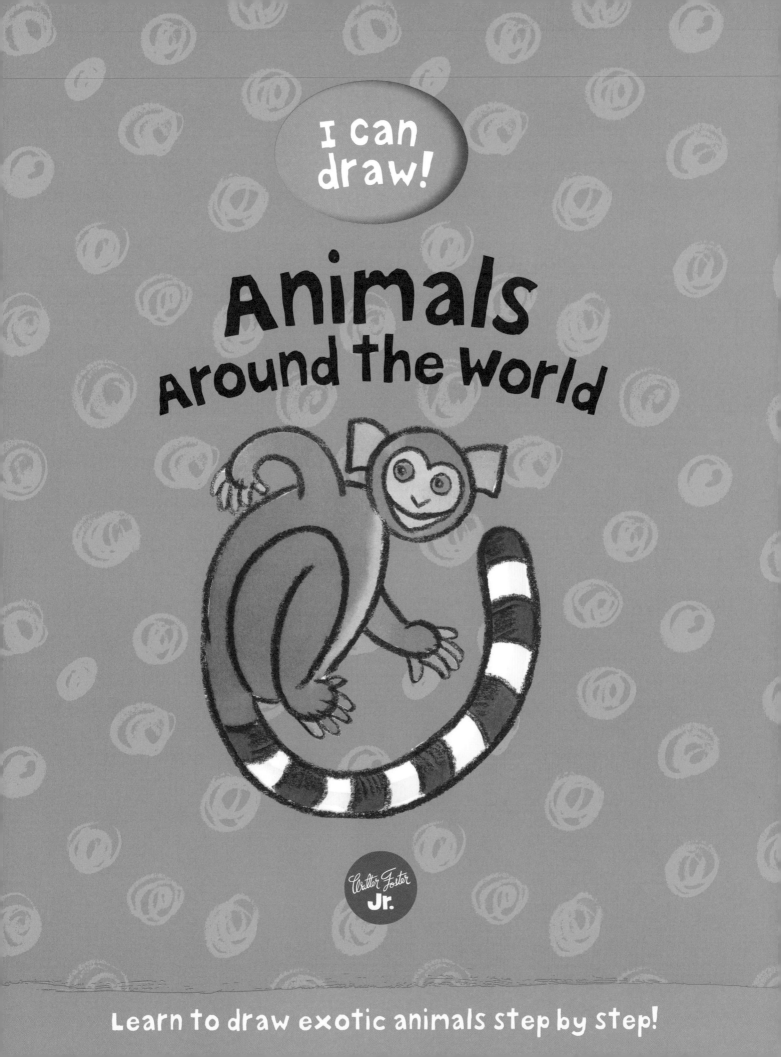

Published by Walter Foster Jr.,
an imprint of Quarto Publishing Group USA Inc.

Illustrated by Philippe Legendre
Written by Janessa Osle

6 Orchard Road, Suite 100
Lake Forest, CA 92630
quartoknows.com
Visit our blogs @quartoknows.com

Printed in China

5 7 9 10 8 6

Table of Contents

Tools & Materials

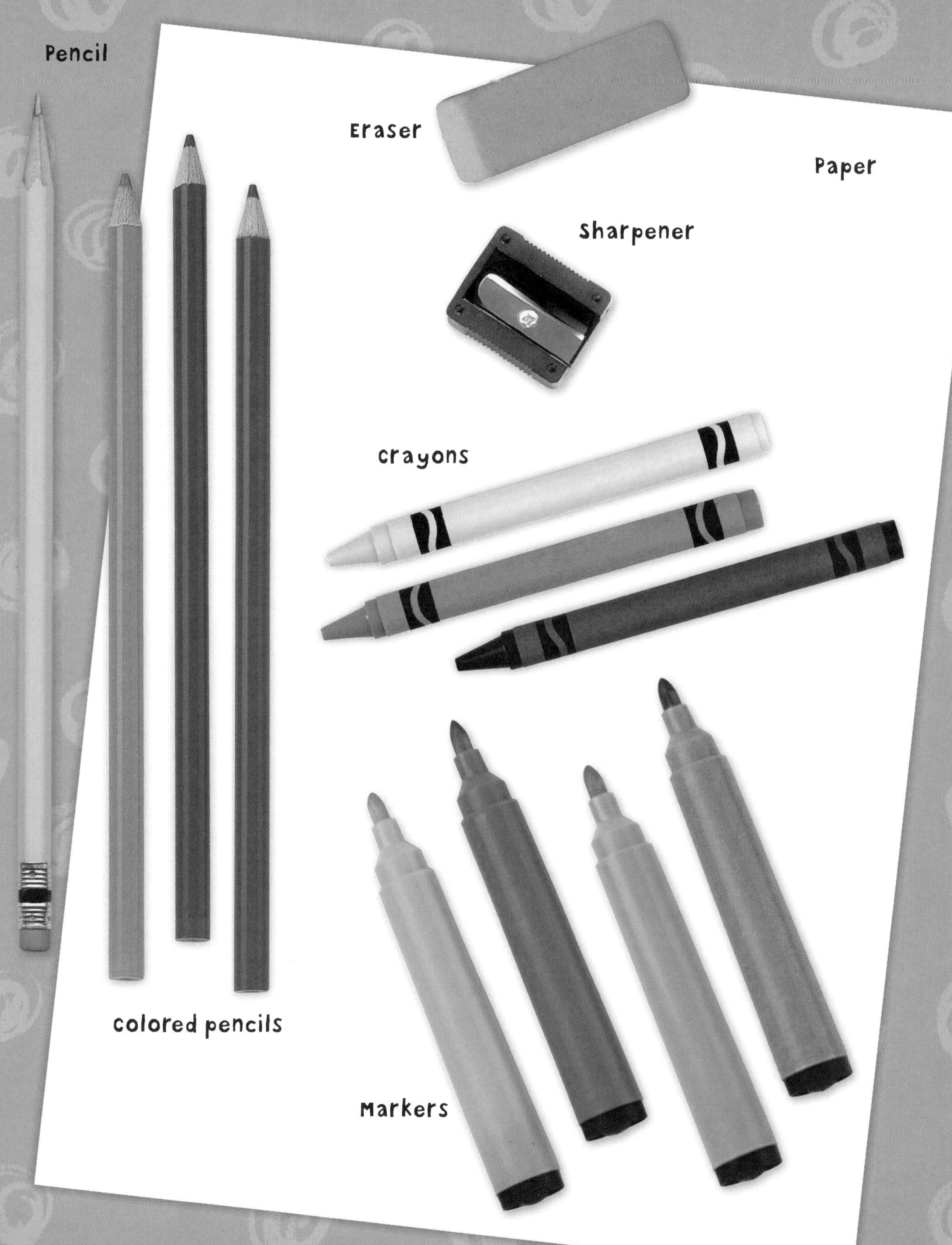

The Color Wheel

The color wheel shows the relationships between colors. It helps us understand how the different colors relate to and react with one another. It's easy to make your own color wheel!

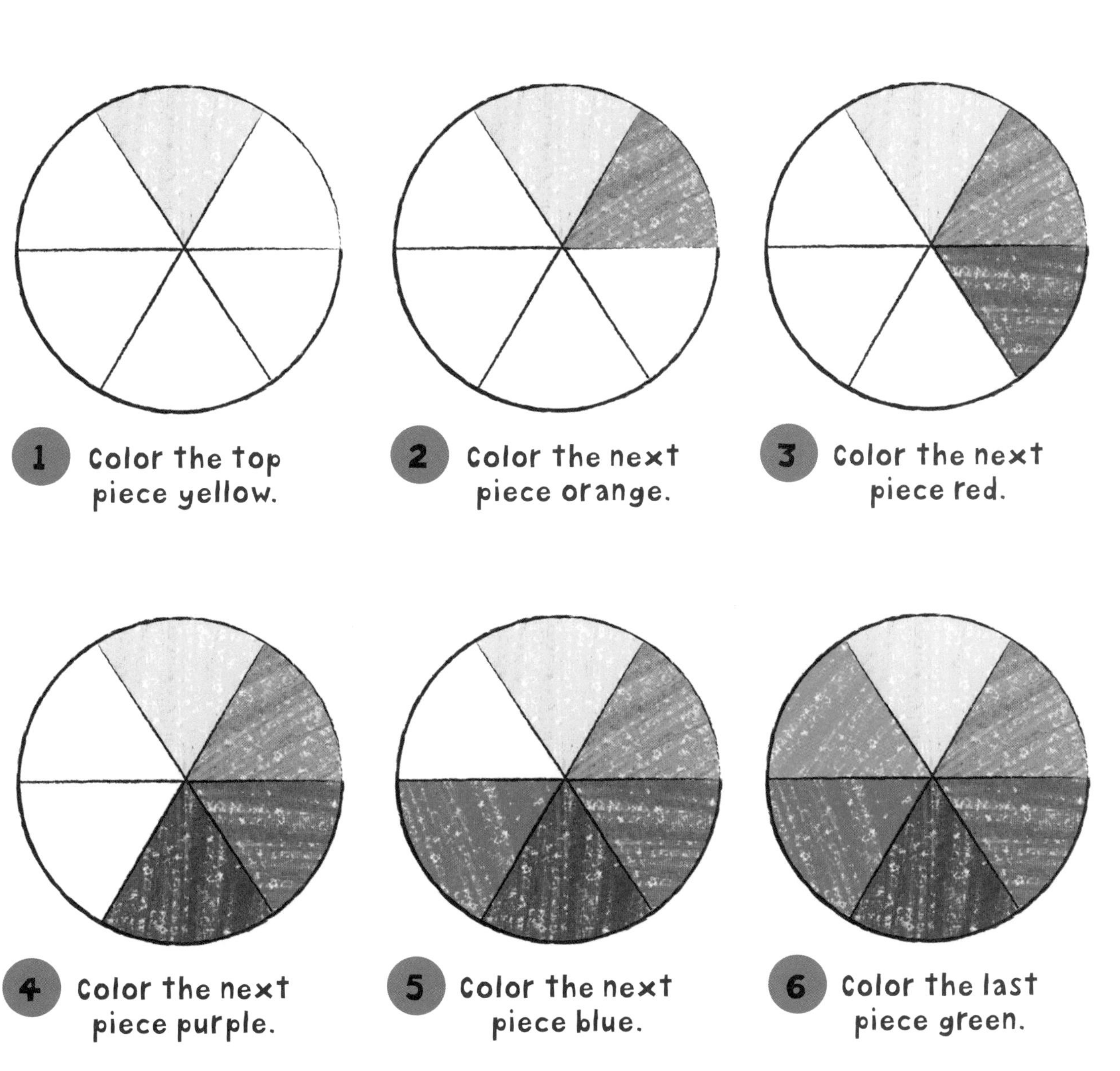

1. Color the top piece yellow.
2. Color the next piece orange.
3. Color the next piece red.
4. Color the next piece purple.
5. Color the next piece blue.
6. Color the last piece green.

Getting Started

Warm up your hand by drawing some squiggles and shapes on a piece of scrap paper.

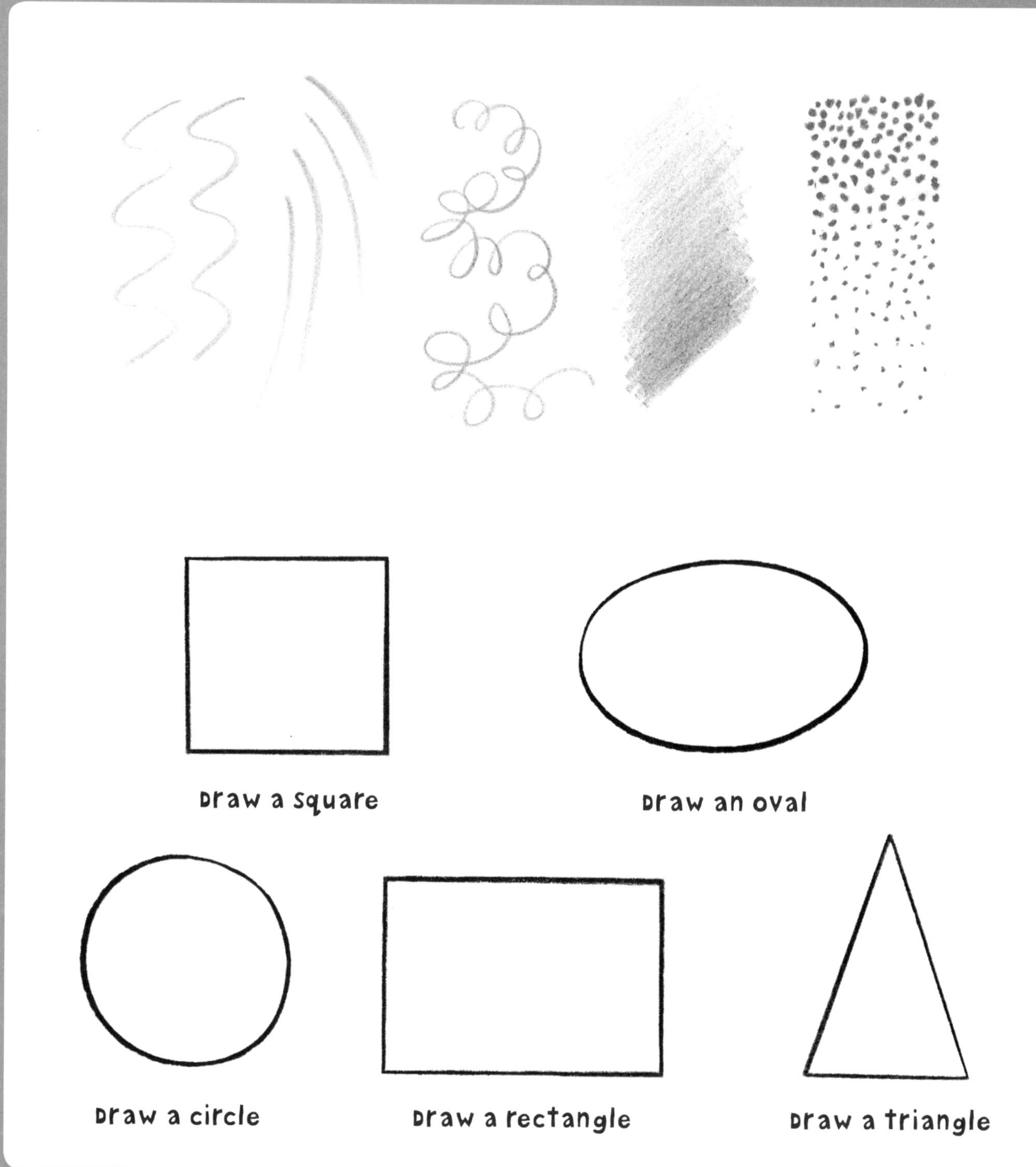
Draw a square
Draw an oval
Draw a circle
Draw a rectangle
Draw a triangle

If you can draw a few basic shapes, you can draw just about anything!

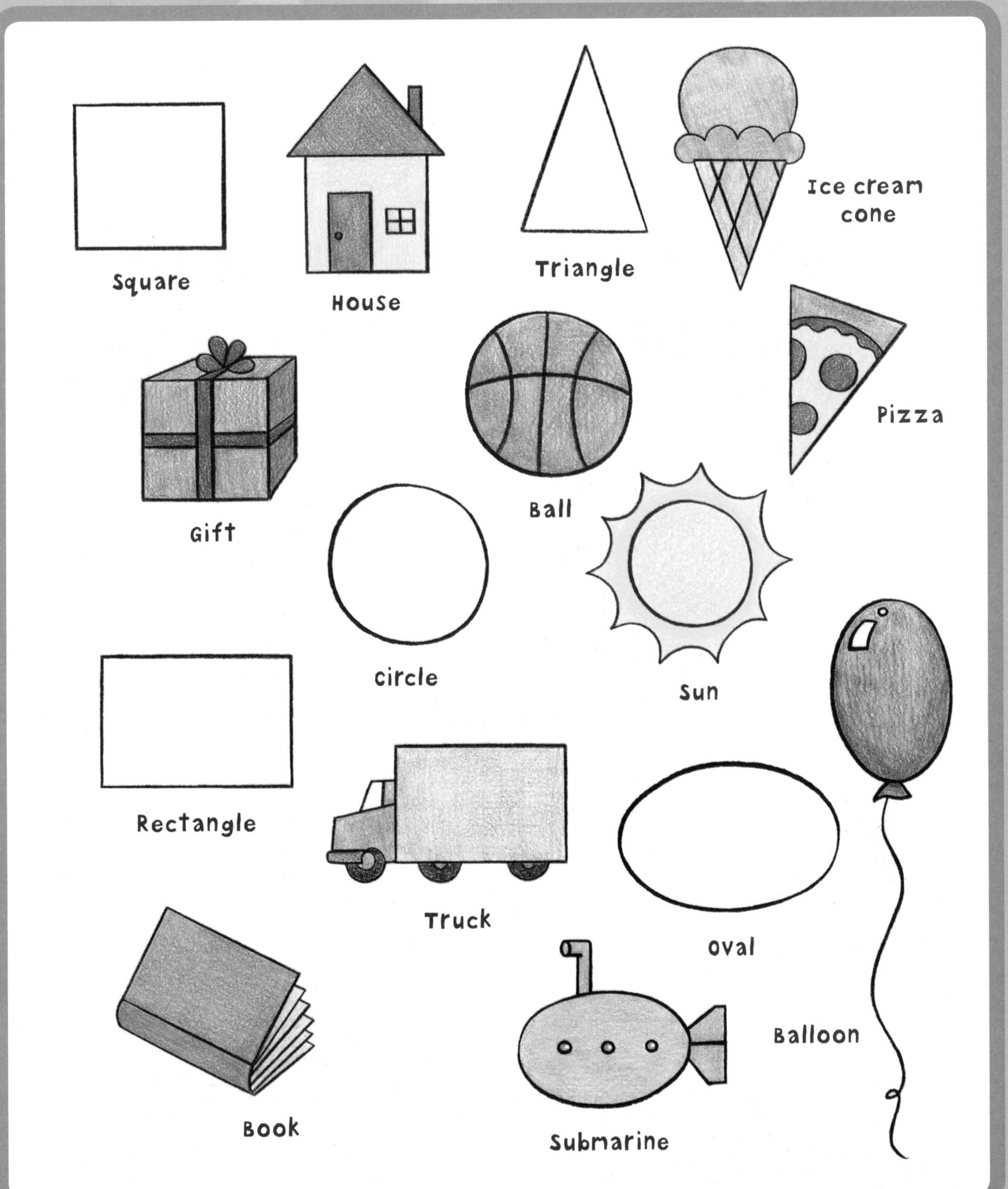

Panda

This bear is black and white and likes to eat bamboo!

1
2
3
4

Camel

This mammal from Africa and Asia can go for long periods of time without drinking water.

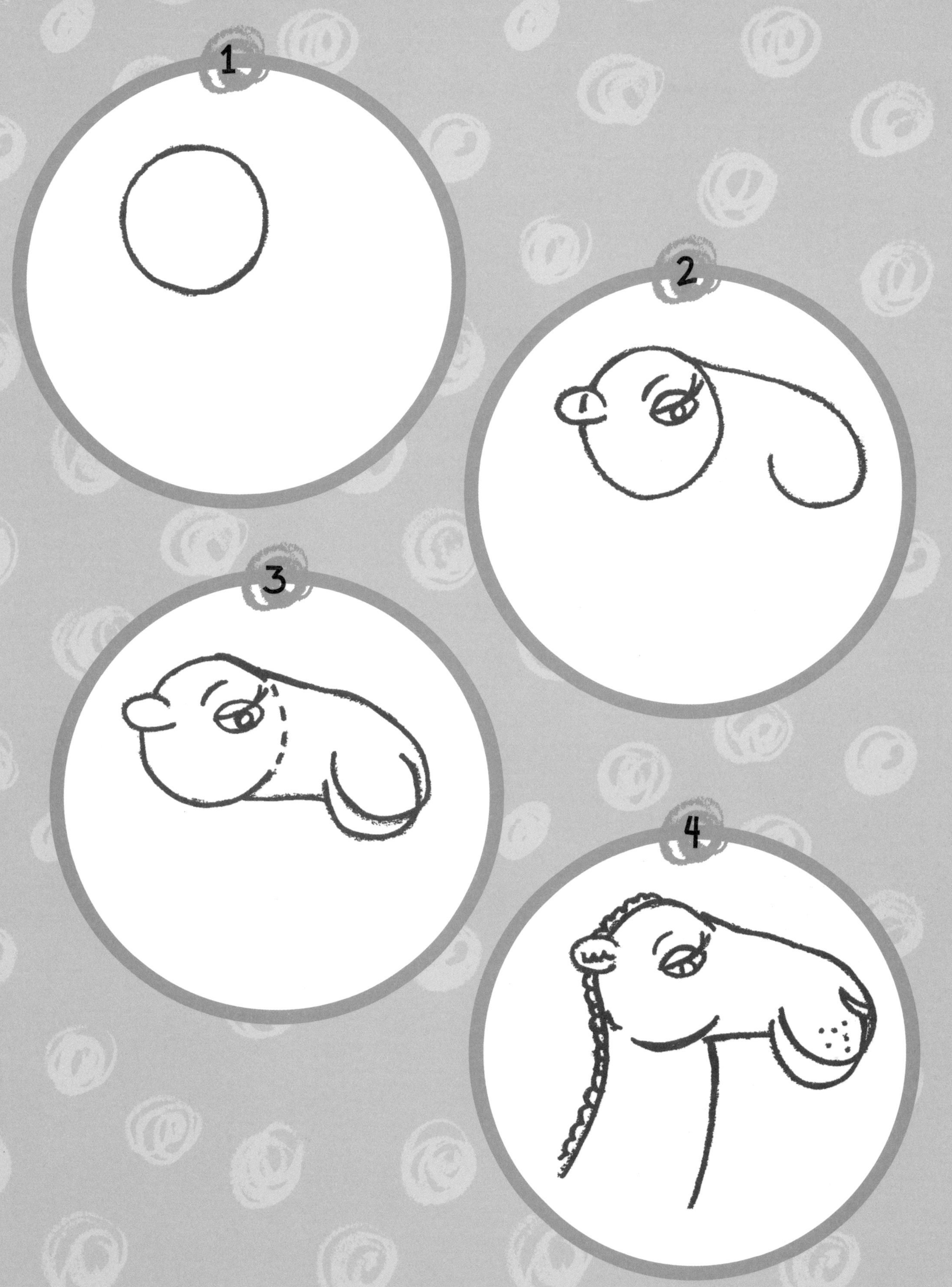
1
2
3
4

Tiger

The tiger is the largest member of the cat family.

1
2
3
4

Bison

This large, powerful animal likes to graze all day!

1
2
3
4

Raccoon

This scavenger will eat almost anything it can find!

1
2
3
4

Kangaroo

This marsupial likes to hop around on its hind legs!

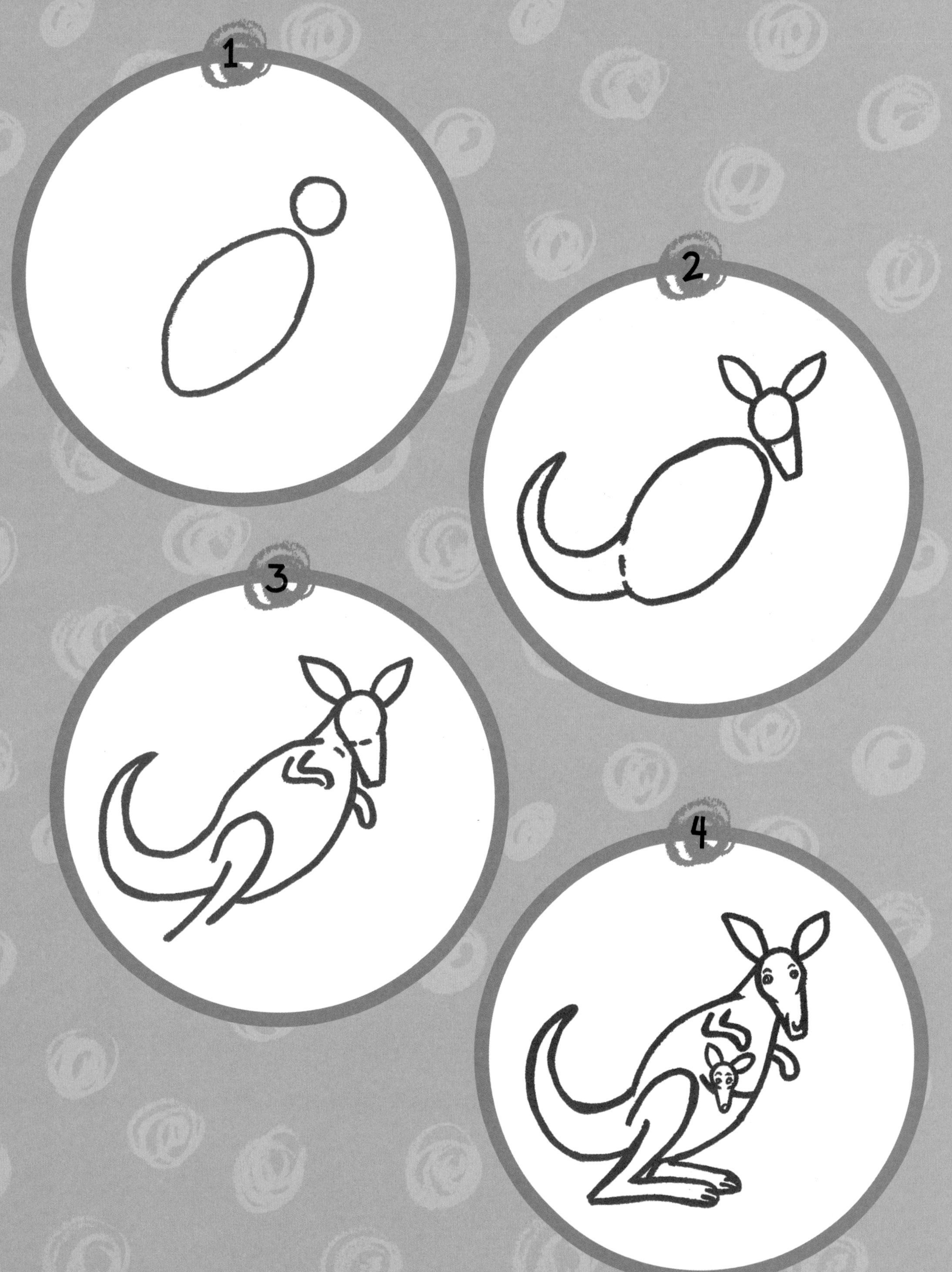
1
2
3
4

Koala

A koala enjoys hanging out in trees and eating eucalyptus leaves.

1
2
3
4

Marmoset

This long-tailed monkey likes to scurry along branches!

1
2
3
4

Cheetah

The cheetah is the fastest land mammal on earth and can run up to 60 miles per hour!

1
2
3
4

Lion

Male lions grow long manes of hair around their heads.

1
2
3
4

Hippopotamus

Hippos love to sleep and play in the water!

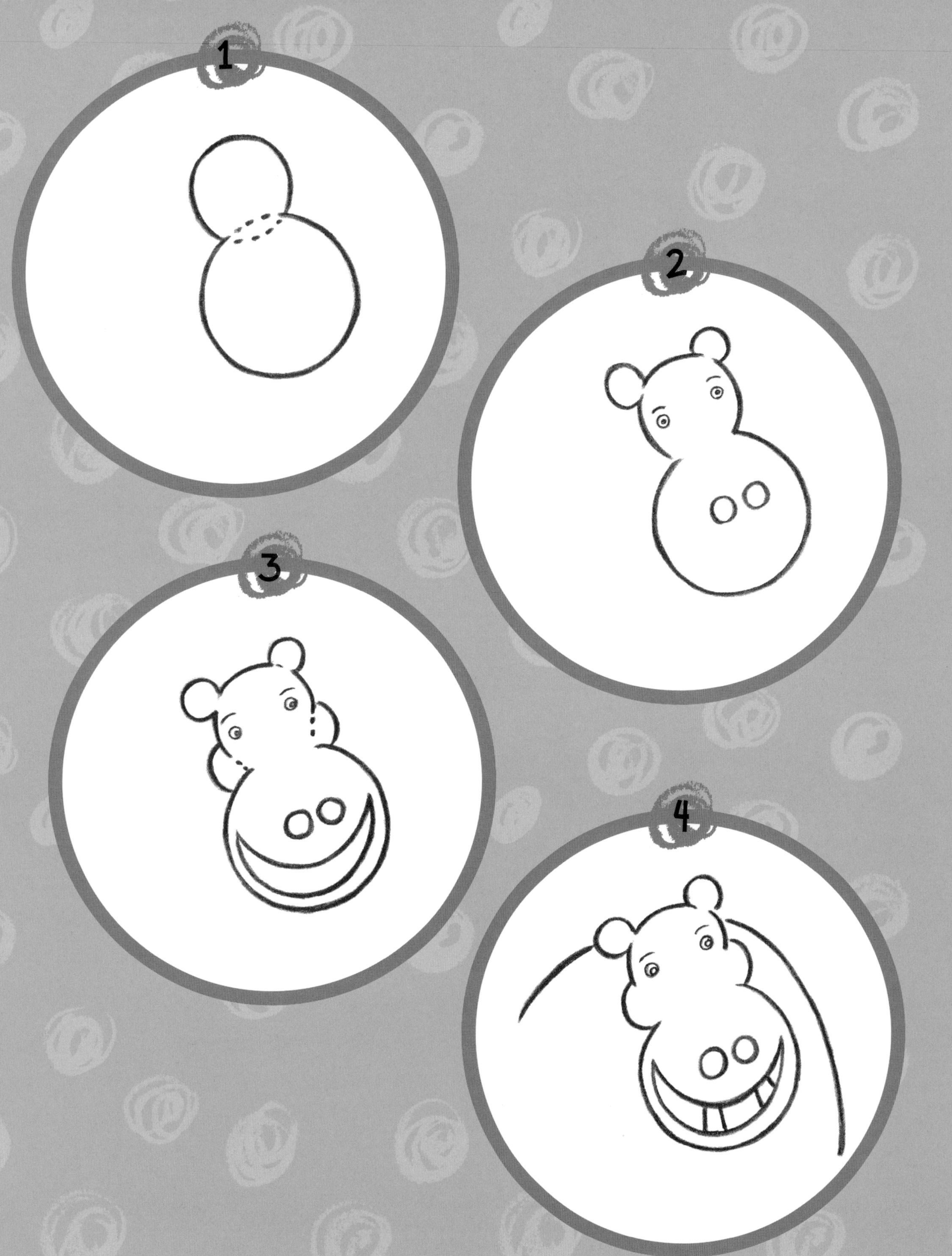
1
2
3
4

Crocodile

This large reptile can hide its whole body underwater while keeping its eyes, ears, and nostrils above the surface.

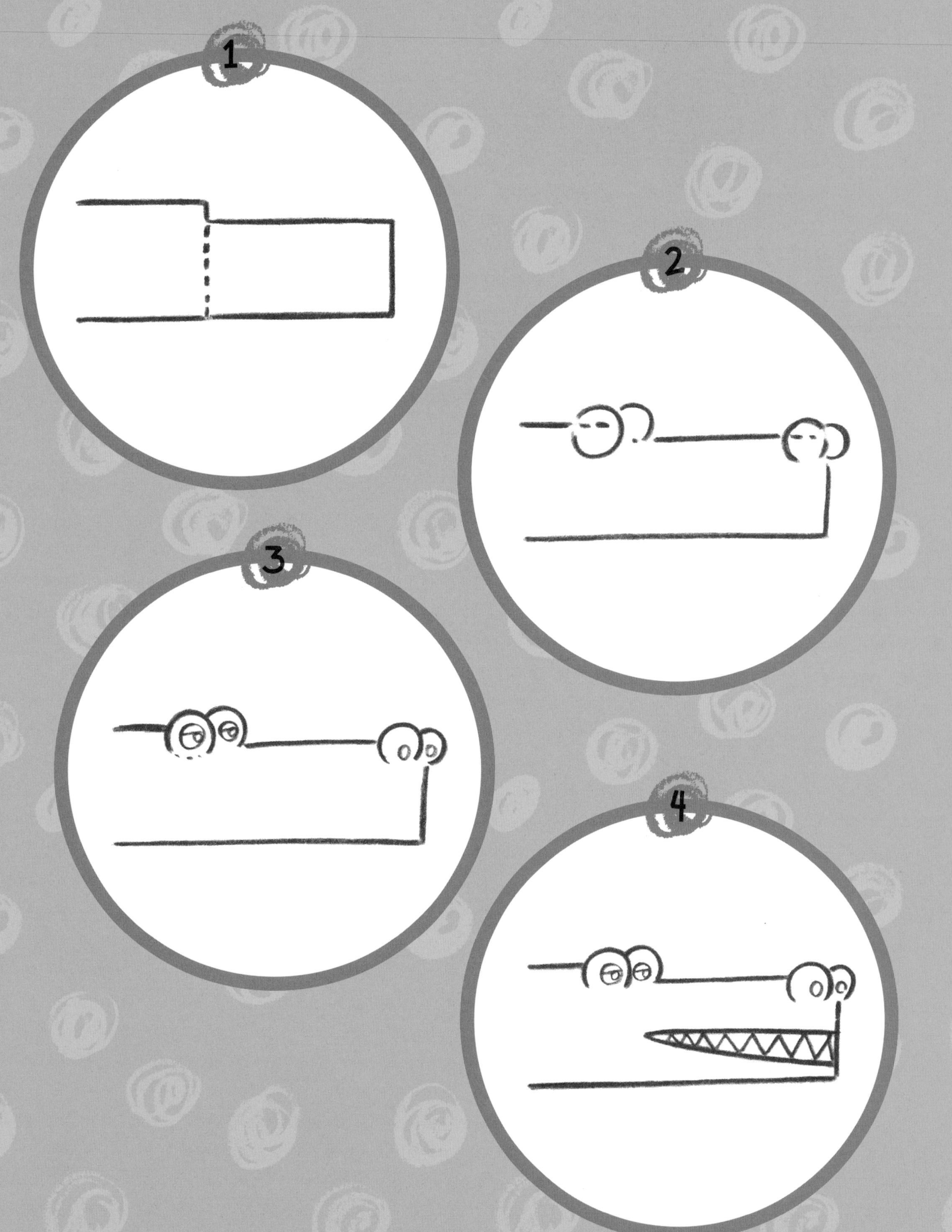
1
2
3
4

Elephant

The elephant is the largest living land animal!

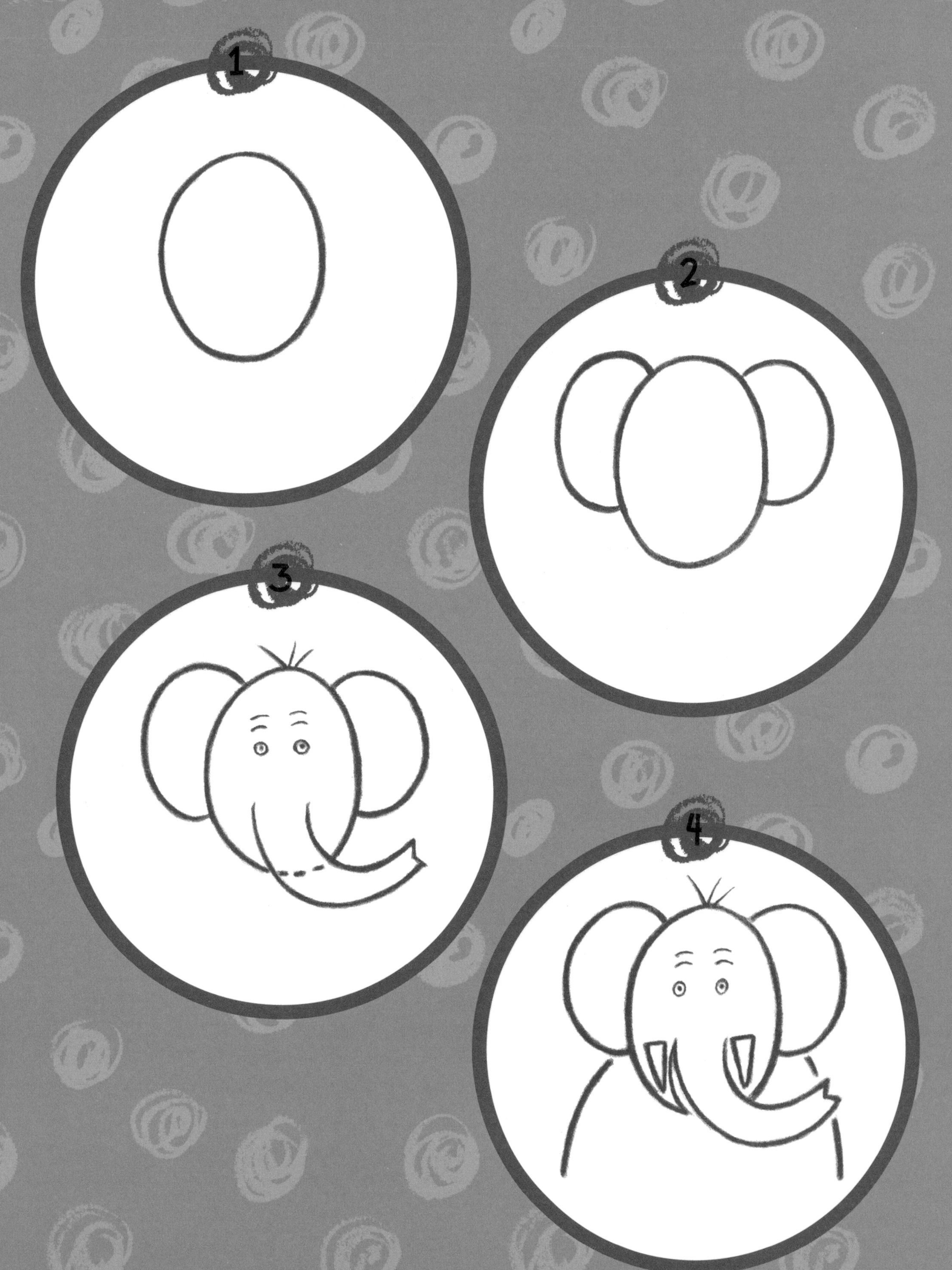
1
2
3
4

Giraffe

The tallest of all land animals, giraffes use their long tongues to eat leaves from treetops!

1
2
3
4

Rhinoceros

This giant herbivore has two horns on top of its snout!

1
2
3
4

Zebra

The zebra is known for the black-and-white stripes on its body.

1
2
3
4

Bear

Bears love to eat honey and berries, among other things!

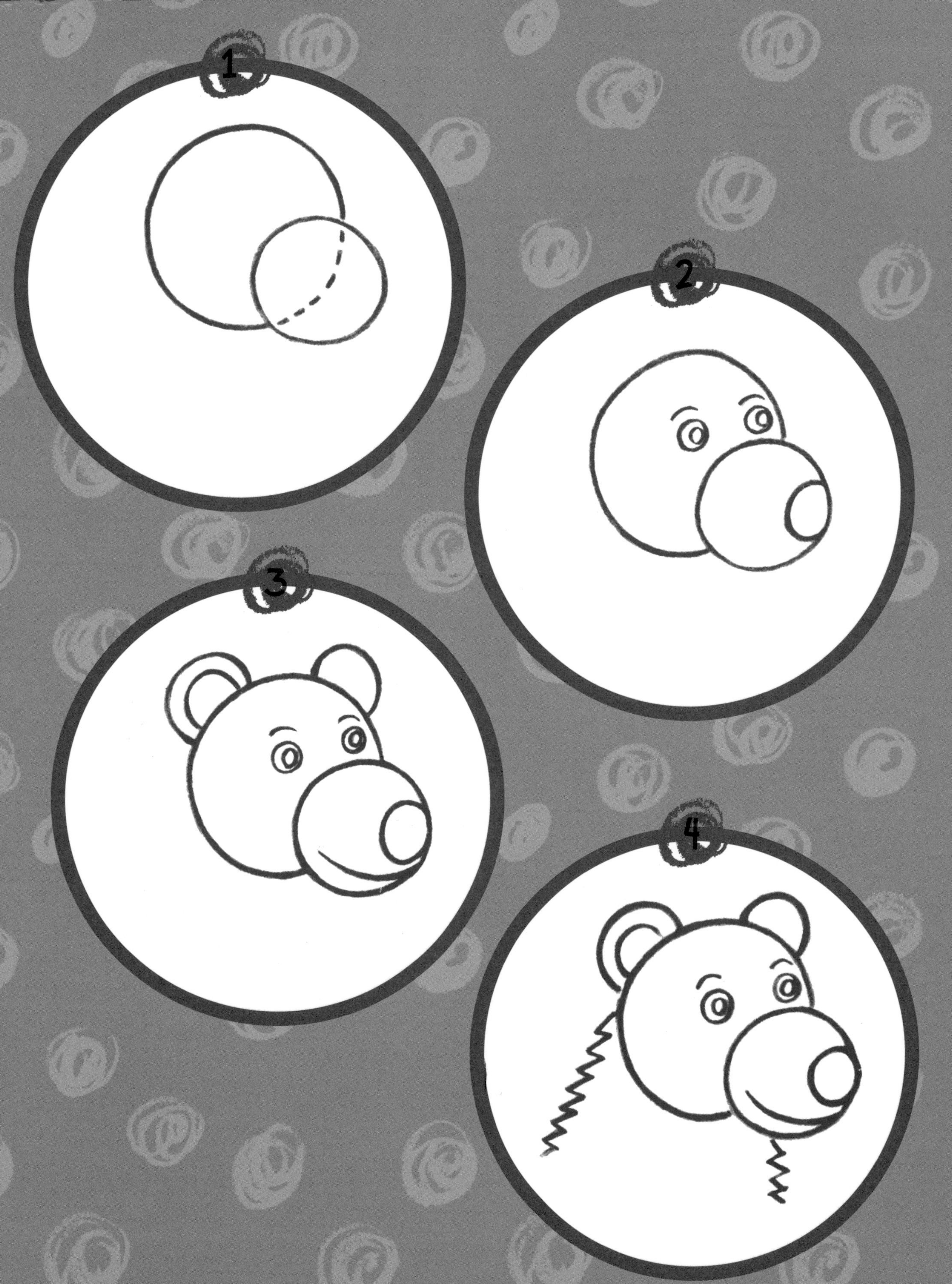
1
2
3
4

Hedgehog

This cute hedgehog has thousands of short, smooth spines all over its body!

1
2
3
4

FOX

The clever fox uses its long, bushy tail to keep warm in the winter.

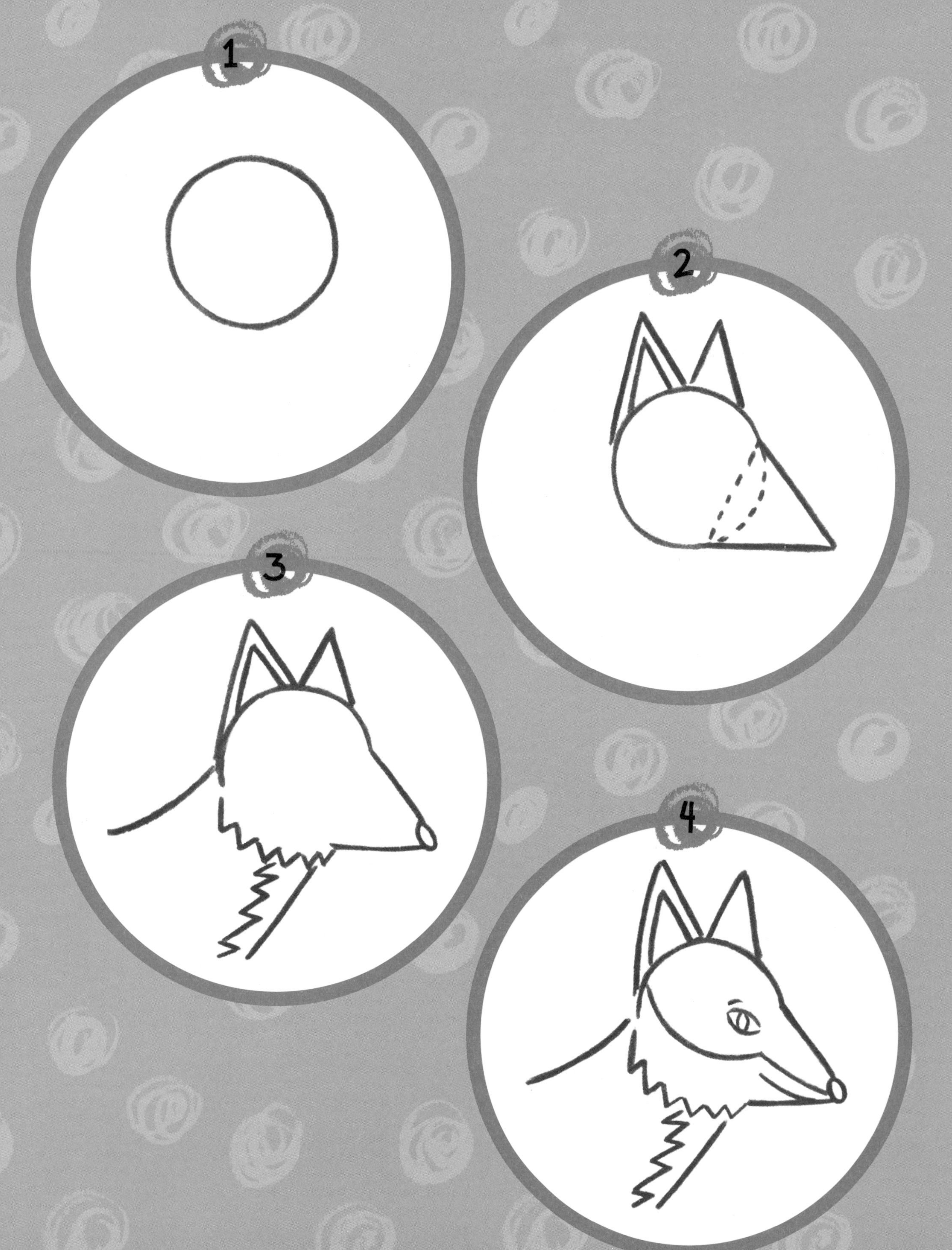
1
2
3
4

The End